STEM
ON THE BATTLEFIELD

HOVERCRAFTS AND HUMVEES
ENGINEERING GOES TO WAR

Terry Burrows

Lerner Publications ◆ Minneapolis

Lerner Publications Company
A division of Lerner Publishing Group, Inc.
241 First Avenue North
Minneapolis, MN 55401 USA

For reading levels and more information, look up this title at www.lernerbooks.com.

Main body text set in Verdana Regular 11/16.5.
Typeface provided by Microsoft.

Picture Credits:
Front Cover: ©Department of Defense.
Interior: ©SVSimigary/Shutterstock, 1; ©Robert Hunt Library, 4; ©Dorling Kindersley/Thinkstock 5; ©Zebra0209/Shutterstock, 6; ©Anna Jurkova/Shutterstock, 7; ©Snowmanradio, 8; ©Michael Conrad/Shutterstock, 9; ©Michael Rosskothen/Shutterstock, 10; ©techotr/Getty Images, 11; ©Rikard Stadier/Shutterstock, 12; ©Robert Hunt Library, 13; ©Dorling Kindersley/Thinkstock, 14; © James Steidl/Shutterstock, 15; ©iStock/Thinkstock, 16; ©Robert Hunt Library, 17tr, 17bl; ©Mar.k/Shutterstock, 18; ©Jakub Krechowicz/Shutterstock, 19tr; ©Robert Hunt Library, 19br; ©Library of Congress, 20; ©Central Naval Museum, St Petersburg, 21; ©Mar.k/Shutterstock, 22; ©Imperial War Museum, 23; ©Library of Congress, 24; ©Everett Historical/Shutterstock, 25; ©Paul Drabot/Shutterstock, 26; ©Nick Whittle/Shutterstock, 27; ©Robert Hunt Library, 28, 29tr, 29br, 30, 31; ©Mary Evans Picture Library, 32; ©Robert Hunt Library, 33tr; Popperfoto/Getty Images, 33cr; ©Robert Hunt Library, 34; ©SVSimigary/Shutterstock, 35; ©Claudiadivizia/Dreamstime, 36; ©Maxal TamarShutterstock, 37tr; ©Robert Hunt Library, 37br; ©National Archives, 38; ©Department of Defense, 39; ©Robert Hunt Library, 40; ©Department of Defense, 41, 42, 43.
Brown Bear Books has made every attempt to contact the copyright holder.
If you have any information please contact licensing@brownbearbooks.co.uk

Library of Congress Cataloging-in-Publication Data

Names: Burrows, Terry, 1963– author.
Title: Hovercraft and humvees : engineering goes to war / Terry Burrows.
Description: Minneapolis : Lerner Publications, [2017] | Series: STEM on the battlefield | Includes bibliographical references and index. | Audience: Grades 4–6. | Audience: Ages 9–12.
Identifiers: LCCN 2016052497 (print) | LCCN 2016052954 (ebook) | ISBN 9781512439298 (lb : alk. paper) | ISBN 9781512449518 (eb pdf)
Subjects: LCSH: Military art and science—History—Juvenile literature. | Military weapons—History—Juvenile literature. | Military vehicles—History—Juvenile literature.
Classification: LCC U27 .B84 2017 (print) | LCC U27 (ebook) | DDC 623—dc23

LC record available at https://lccn.loc.gov/2016052497

Manufactured in the United States of America
1-42142-25415-3/14/2017

CONTENTS

ENGINEERING AT WAR

In June 1944 British and US soldiers began the biggest invasion in history. The invasion was called D-Day. For most of World War II (1939–1945), France had been occupied by German forces. More than 150,000 **Allied** troops landed in France on June 6. They needed supplies, but there were no harbors for supply ships. Allied engineers built massive floating harbors, called Mulberry harbors. These were towed to France from Britain and were operational within a few days. They helped the invasion to succeed.

CLOSE CONNECTION

Engineering is the technology of designing, building, and using engines, machines, and structures such as roads or **fortifications**.

Part of a Mulberry harbor is towed to France on D-Day. Together, the two floating harbors were about 5 miles (8 kilometers) long.

The word *engineer* began as a military term. In the fourteenth century, an "engine'er" built machines such as catapults and battering rams. These machines were all called engines.

ADVANCING TECHNOLOGY

Warfare has often led to advances in engineering. World War I (1914–1918) led to the invention of radio communication. World War II saw the development of radio navigation, jet engines, and the atom bomb. After World War II, the United States tried to gain more influence in the world than the Soviet Union, a **communist** country based in modern Russia that existed from 1922 to 1991. The struggle between them was known as the Cold War (1947–1991). It led to one of humankind's greatest feats of engineering—space travel.

Medieval soldiers use a catapult, battering ram, and cannons to attack a castle. These devices were all known as engines.

ROMAN ROADS

The first people to use engineering to support their army were the ancient Romans. Roman engineers constructed buildings, roads, and bridges.

Between the third century BCE and the end of the first century CE, Roman armies controlled most of Europe and North Africa. Rome's expansion relied on its armies being able to move quickly by ship or on land. Roman legions, or groups of soldiers, built new roads as they advanced into new lands.

Roman soldiers were carved on an arch celebrating a Roman victory in 315 CE.

The roads helped the Romans to move **reinforcements** and supplies quickly, even to faraway locations.

BUILDING A ROAD

Roman roads were as straight as possible, so legions could march between two points quickly. These roads also provided fewer hiding places for enemies or bandits.

Roman roads survive all over Rome's old empire. They are easy to identify because they are usually straight and made of stone.

Every legion was accompanied by a **surveyor**. His job was to plan the route of the road. He used a *groma* to find flat terrain. A groma was a wooden cross with weights hanging from it. The surveyor then marked the path the road should take with wooden stakes for builders to follow.

BUILDING FORTS

Military surveyors built forts in remote parts of the empire. The forts had defensive walls made of wood or stone to protect the soldiers from attack. Inside the walls, the streets and blocks followed a grid pattern. There were blocks for soldiers, bathhouses, and stores. Buildings were laid out in the same way in every fort.

This wooden gateway guarded a Roman fort at Lunt, in central England. The upper floor was used by soldiers to keep watch for attackers.

The shape of a small fort stands next to Hadrian's Wall in northern England.

Hadrian's Wall

Hadrian's Wall was the largest structure built in the Roman Empire. The stone wall was 73 miles (117 km) long, and was around 15 feet (4.6 m) high and 10 feet (3 m) wide. It took 15,000 men six years to build the wall. There were dozens of forts along the wall. Small forts were built every Roman mile (about 0.92 miles, or 1.48 km). Each small fort held 20 to 30 men. Larger forts were built every five Roman miles (4.6 miles, or 7.4 km).

EDGE OF THE EMPIRE

In some places, Roman engineers built walls to defend the edges of the empire. One of the most famous examples was Hadrian's Wall in northern Britain. Roman Emperor Hadrian ordered the construction of this wall in 122 CE. He wanted to protect Roman territory from attack by the Picts, a Celtic people who lived to the north in modern Scotland.

GALLEYS AND GALLEONS

For about 4,000 years, humans have waged war at sea. Military engineers designed and built warships that used the power of the wind and of human labor.

The first fighting ships were built by early peoples. The Minoans lived in Crete from around 2000 BCE. They built warships to protect their territory and trade. These early warships, called galleys, were propelled through the water by a large crew of rowers. The most powerful type of galley was known as a trireme. It had three banks of rowers on each side.

This replica of a trireme shows the banks of oars and the ram on the waterline at the front of the ship.

collar (fulcrum)

In a rowboat, the oars act as levers. The lever helps the rowers generate force to move the boat through the water.

oar (lever)

paddle in water (force)

GALLEY CONSTRUCTION

The construction of galleys took great skill. The ships needed to be strong and fast but easy to steer and stable enough to carry dozens of men. The ships were up to 120 feet (36.6 m) long, made of fir, pine, and cedar wood.

Galleys were used to attack other vessels. Long, sharp points called rams were fitted at the waterline at the pointed front of galleys. In battle, they were rammed into the sides of enemy vessels to damage them. Galleys also carried armed soldiers. If the galley came close to an enemy ship, soldiers with swords jumped onboard the other ship.

Oars and Levers

In China, oars have been used to power vessels since around 5000 BCE. Oars act as levers. Each oar is held in place at the side of the vessel by a collar that acts as a fulcrum. Pulling on the oar works against the fulcrum to create a force that pushes against the water. This propels the vessel forward.

The sails on a sailing ship can be arranged across the width of the vessel, as shown here. They can also be turned to face almost sideways along the ship to catch the wind.

Sailing into the Wind

Sailing ships changed direction when sailors adjusted the position of the sails. The sails were attached to the masts on horizontal beams called yards. They were swung around by ropes at the end of the yards called braces. Turning the sails almost sideways along the length of the ship allowed ships to sail almost directly into the wind.

SAILING SHIPS

The last major clash between galleys was the Battle of Lepanto near Greece in 1571. European nations defeated the Ottoman empire, which was based in modern Turkey. For the next three centuries, ships powered by sails were dominant. In the fifteenth century, the Portuguese built a type of large sailing ship called a carrack. It was designed to carry heavy cargo on long journeys.

By the early sixteenth century, these large carracks were sailing from Europe to India, China, and South America.

AGE OF GALLEONS

Countries such as Spain, France, and England began to build heavily armed, **multi-decked** sailing warships called galleons. They were effective in sea battles. In 1534 the Portuguese built the galleon *Botofogo*. This ship had 366 cannons and was the biggest sea vessel of its time. The Battle of Trafalgar (1805) between the British and French and Spanish navies was the last great naval conflict of the sailing ship era. Within a few years, engineers had created the first steam-powered armor-plated warships.

During the Battle of Trafalgar, galleons tried to sail alongside enemy ships. This tactic allowed them to fire all the cannons on one side of the ship at the same time.

CASTLES AND DEFENSES

In the Middle Ages rulers or nobles built many castles. Castles protected those inside from attack. They also helped display the owner's rank and wealth.

The first castles were built in Europe and the Middle East in the ninth century. They were called motte and bailey castles. A motte was a mound made out of earth. On top of the motte stood a wooden or stone tower known as a keep. This was where the occupants of the castle lived. The bailey was an enclosed courtyard built at the foot of the motte. It had room for **barracks**, kitchens, stables, **forges**, and workshops.

Some motte and bailey castles were surrounded by a moat, or water-filled ditch, for added protection from attack.

BIGGER CASTLES

Nobles soon built bigger castles. The walls became taller and thicker. Engineers added towers along the walls. By the twelfth century the towers were usually round instead of square. Square towers collapsed more easily if the enemy dug holes beneath the corners. Archers stood in the towers to fire down at attackers outside the walls.

At the top of the walls and towers were the battlements, or fortified walkways. Defenders there fired **missiles** at the enemy below through tooth-shaped gaps in the battlements called crenels.

The arm of a trebuchet was pulled down to create tension. The missile was loaded. When the tension was released, weights at the front of the arm swung it rapidly up, throwing the missile forward.

The raised sections between the gaps were called merlons. These protected the defenders during an attack. Castles were often surrounded by moats filled with water, which made them easier to defend. The drawbridge across the moat to the castle entrance could be pulled up to stop enemies from entering the castle.

STRONGER CASTLES

The great era of castle building in Europe was during the twelfth and thirteenth centuries. At the time, Europe's rulers were fighting in many conflicts. Engineers built fewer motte and bailey castles. European armies had just begun to use **artillery** powered by gunpowder, and cannonballs easily destroyed old castle walls.

The castle at Manzanares el Real was built near Madrid in Spain in 1475. Its walls have battlements and circular towers. It was hard to attack.

New castles were built entirely of stone. They had stronger fortifications. Star-shaped walls protected the castles. Sets of parallel walls all followed the same pattern, one inside the other. This created many barriers for attackers.

By the seventeenth century, castles no longer had a military purpose. Many were converted to law courts or government offices. Wealthy nobles abandoned their castles in favor of new country houses. These houses were not built for defense but to show off the owner's wealth.

This design is for a star fort in Slovakia. The star-shaped walls have towers surrounded by earth banks. The banks absorbed enemy cannon fire before it could destroy the castle walls.

LEONARDO'S WEAPONS

Leonardo da Vinci was a leading figure of the Italian Renaissance, a period of great advances in the arts and sciences. Da Vinci was a famous artist, but he was also an inventor and a military engineer.

Few of da Vinci's inventions were ever built. But some were similar to weapons that would be created many centuries later. In 1487 he designed an armored vehicle similar to a tank. It was moved by turning a crank. In 1481 he invented a cannon with three barrels. He later came up with an early type of machine gun with thirty-three barrels. (The first actual machine gun was not made for another 300 years.)

This model is based on da Vinci's design for an armored vehicle made from a wheeled cart inside a wooden shell.

MILITARY DESIGNS

While he was working for the Duke of Milan, da Vinci designed a military swing bridge that could be packed up and moved around. It was put across streams or moats to allow troops to cross.

Da Vinci also designed the first plan for a manned flying machine, or ornithopter. Da Vinci studied the flight of birds to come up with his design. His plan featured flapping wings to power the machine. He also designed a type of helicopter and the first parachute.

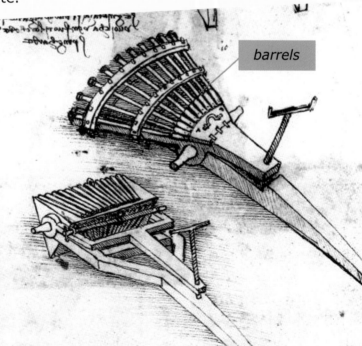

barrels

Da Vinci's military designs included a number of weapons with many barrels that could fire rapidly, like a modern machine gun.

THE NEW WARSHIPS

In the nineteenth century, steam engines powered ships made of iron and steel. This led to new ways of fighting at sea.

The first steam warships were built in Europe in the 1820s. This was during a period called the Industrial Revolution, when engineers invented new machines to perform many tasks. New factories mass-produced iron and steel to make new machines. **Steam engines** powered locomotives and ships. Steam engines turned **propellers** that pushed ships through the water. They generated power by burning coal.

The Battle of Hampton Roads, Virginia, took place in March 1862, during the US Civil War (1861–1865). The battle was the first time two iron-covered ships fought each other.

At the Battle of Sinop, Russian cannons destroyed the Turkish fleet. The Turkish defeat showed that wooden warships were of little use against cannons.

Coal was not available in some parts of the world, however, so steam ships also had a full set of sails.

EXPLOSIVE SHELLS

Explosive cannon shells were also invented during this time. The Battle of Sinop took place in the Black Sea near Turkey in 1853. The Russian navy used explosive shells to destroy the wooden ships of the Ottoman Empire.

SHIPS OF IRON

The Battle of Sinop changed warship construction. Engineers protected the wooden hulls of ships with armor plates made from iron. The first of these warships, known as ironclads, fought in the Civil War. Union forces from the North fought southern Confederate forces. In 1861 the Confederate ironclad ship CSS *Manassas* attacked Union ships at the Battle of the Head of Passes in Louisiana.

Submarines

In 1775 the engineer David Bushnell designed the first submarine. He named it the *Turtle*. Bushnell planned to use it to attach underwater bombs to British ships during the Revolutionary War (1775–1783). In 1864, during the Civil War, the submersible *H.L. Hunley* sank the Union ship *Housatonic*. It was during World War I that the submarine first had a real impact. German submarines called U-boats sank British and US supply ships in the Atlantic.

A soldier named Ezra Lee tried to use Turtle to attach explosives to British ships. He gave up when he became exhausted from turning the crank to propel the vessel.

The British Royal Navy launched HMS Dreadnought in 1906. The British then built many identical ships, known as the Dreadnoughts.

By the end of the 1860s, steel began to replace iron in warships. Steel ships were stronger and far lighter than iron. By the end of the nineteenth century, most warships were made from steel.

THE BATTLESHIP

Steel made it easier to build larger warships. In 1892, the British Royal Navy gave the powerful steel ships the name *battleship*. The first modern battleship was called HMS *Dreadnought*, which was launched in 1906. It was powered by four steam turbines. Its 12-inch guns could fire shells over 11 miles (17.5 km). The *Dreadnought* made all existing battleships **obsolete**.

WARPLANES

Aerial warfare is ancient. Over 2,000 years ago, the Chinese military used kites to send signals. The modern era of flight began when the Montgolfier brothers launched the first hot-air balloon in France.

In 1794 the French founded the world's first air force. It used hot-air balloons. That same year, the French watched the enemy from balloons at the Battle of Fleurus in the French Revolutionary Wars (1792–1802). In the US Civil War, the Union used balloons to observe Confederate positions.

The Wright Brothers built the first airplane in 1903. A motor turned propellers to push it forward. In 1910 the US Navy experimented with shooting guns from an airplane.

The American balloonist Thaddeus Lowe begins a balloon flight to examine enemy positions during the US Civil War.

A year later, Italian pilots dropped bombs by hand on Turkish troops during a war between Italy and Turkey.

WORLD WAR I

World War I was the first time large numbers of aircraft were used in warfare. Pilots flew monoplanes, which had only one set of wings, or biplanes with two pairs of wings stacked on top of each other.

Thaddeus Lowe

(1832–1913) was a self-taught US inventor. In the 1850s, he became fascinated by flight. He built his own hot-air balloons. Lowe tried to cross the Atlantic by balloon twice. Both attempts failed. When the Civil War broke out in 1861, Lowe formed the Union Balloon Corps.

An English pilot chases a German biplane in this illustration of a **dogfight** during World War I.

The most famous pilot of the war was the German Baron Manfred von Richthofen. He flew a Fokker triplane like this one.

In 1917, the first triplanes, with three stacked pairs of wings, appeared. They were easier to **maneuver** than biplanes, but they were slower.

WAR IN THE AIR

Pilots used airplanes to observe the enemy. Later, the pilots fought in dogfights. They shot at other pilots with handguns. The handguns were later replaced with machine guns.

In the 1920s and 1930s, aircraft design changed quickly. Air forces replaced biplanes with stronger, metal-framed

SCIENCE FILE

Monoplanes and Biplanes

In World War I, aircraft engines were not yet very powerful. That meant that to lift off the ground, airplanes needed a large wing surface. In a monoplane, the large single wings became weak. They sometimes snapped. The biplane's double wings lifted the plane more easily. Biplanes were easier to steer than monoplanes. They were also stronger, lighter, and easier to build.

monoplane fighters. Engineers also developed much larger aircraft. These were used as bombers and for transportation. Air warfare played a key role in many battles. In 1940 the British and German air forces, known as the Royal Air Force and the Luftwaffe, fought in the Battle of Britain. This conflict is seen as the first major battle fought entirely in the air.

Technology developed quickly after the war. The invention of the jet engine gave birth to a new generation of powerful fighter planes.

British engineer Reginald J. Mitchell designed the Supermarine Spitfire, one of the most famous fighter planes of World War II. It had a top speed of 350 mph (595 km/h).

THE FIRST TANKS

Engineers added engines and armor to military vehicles in the early twentieth century. But these changes made vehicles so heavy they sank in soft ground.

One solution was to replace the vehicles' wheels with continuous tracks made from steel plates. The large surface area of the tracks distributed the weight of the vehicle more evenly than wheels. This stopped the vehicle from sinking into soft ground.

A British engineer tests a vehicle with tracks in World War I. Engineers tried to figure out the best way to steer the vehicles.

EARLY TESTS

The idea of tracked vehicles began in the late eighteenth century. It was not until 1901 that a practical all-terrain vehicle was produced. It was a tractor used to drag logs through the forest.

In 1905 the British Army tested a tracked tractor. They decided it had no military use. Soldiers called the vehicle the caterpillar—a name that is still often used to describe tracked vehicles. The first tank, or armored fighting vehicle, was used in World War I.

THE BRAINS

Ernest Swinton
(1868–1951) was a war reporter who inspired the development of the tank. He was alarmed at how many men were being killed by new machine guns in World War I. Swinton got the idea for the tank when he saw a US Holt caterpillar tractor being used to tow a gun. He drew up plans for what became the British Mark I tank.

Canadian soldiers ride on top of a British Mark IV tank in France in 1918, near the end of World War I.

German tanks take part in a victory parade near the Arc de Triomphe in Paris, France, in June 1940. Rapid tank advances helped German soldiers to defeat France in only two months.

In 1916 the British Army used tanks armed with machine guns to fight German troops at the Battle of the Somme in France.

WORLD WAR II

By the start of World War II in 1939, tanks were equipped with a large main gun. Armored vehicles played a major role in the conflict.

In the early part of the war, the German Army used tanks to make rapid advances into enemy territory. The advances were accompanied by fighter aircraft.

OTHER VEHICLES

Other tracked vehicles also appeared in World War II. They included tank destroyers, or tank killers. These special tanks used big guns to put other tanks out of action. Tracked vehicles were also used to carry soldiers. These vehicles included the half-track, which had tracks at the rear but wheels for steering at the front. The half-track could be driven without the special training needed to drive a tank.

US Marines sail an LVT toward Tinian Island in the Pacific in July 1944. US forces invaded Tinian as part of the campaign to capture the Marianas Islands.

Amphibious Vehicles

Amphibious vehicles can operate in water and on land. The first widely used amphibious combat vehicle was the LVT-1. It was first used by the US Navy in 1942 in the Pacific. The vehicle's tracks had ridges called grousers. These pushed the LVT through the water and provided a solid grip as it drove onto the beach.

BOMBERS AND JETS

The first bombers appeared early in World War I. They were designed to attack targets on the ground rather than other aircraft.

The British Bristol TB8 biplane was a World War I bomber. It carried twelve 10-pound (4.5-kilogram) bombs. The aircraft had a bombsight in the cockpit. This device helped the pilot aim his bombs at targets on the ground. The TB8 was too slow for front-line operations, however. The most successful bombers of World War I were **airships** such as the German Zeppelin.

In this illustration, a British artillery gun fires at a German Zeppelin lit up by a spotlight. Airships like the Zeppelin were the most effective bombers of World War I.

The German Stuka was a dive bomber. It approached its target in a vertical dive before dropping its bomb.

LARGER BOMBERS

Between World War I and World War II, engineers started building larger aircraft. These could carry heavier loads of bombs. In 1937, the German Luftwaffe used a tactic called carpet bombing to attack the city of Guernica during the Spanish Civil War (1936–1939). Bombers dropped large numbers of bombs across a wide area. During World War II, British and US aircraft bombed cities in Germany using carpet bombing.

THE BRAINS

Barnes Wallis (1887–1979) was an English engineer who came up with the idea of the "bouncing bomb." Wallis designed the bomb to skim across the surface of the water. The British used this weapon to attack dams in Germany in World War II. The bomb sank and blew up as it reached a dam wall.

The technology of the Boeing B-29 Superfortress was advanced for World War II. The bomber remained in service until 1960.

Bomber technology advanced quickly during World War II. Engineers designed bombers for specific purposes. Small dive bombers dove vertically to bomb their targets. They were used to attack enemy ships. Dive bombers included the American Douglas SBD and German Junkers Stuka, which had bent wings, like a gull.

HEAVY BOMBERS

Engineers built new heavy bombers, including the American Boeing B-29 Superfortress, the most expensive piece of military hardware produced during World War II. It had a **pressurized** cabin, so it could fly higher than other airplanes. It also had a remote firing system so that one gunner could fire four separate machine guns. On August 6, 1945, the B-29 Enola Gay dropped an atomic bomb on the Japanese city of Hiroshima. The bomb destroyed the city and killed at least 90,000 people.

THE AGE OF THE JET

By the end of World War II, aircraft were being built with turbojet engines. The new jet engines were lighter than the old piston engines. This meant engineers could build light airplanes. By the 1950s, jet fighter pilots began to use radar to locate the enemy or to find their targets on the ground. By the 1970s, turbofans had replaced turbojet engines. This led to even greater speeds and better fuel economy.

The Sound Barrier

Sound travels at 768 mph (1,236 km/h). When a jet aircraft flies faster, we say it breaks the sound barrier. The speed is also known as Mach 1. Drops of water from the plane condense and create a white halo, and there is a sonic boom. This explosion is caused by sound waves that have been forced together.

A jet forms a halo of condensed water as it breaks the sound barrier.

HELICOPTERS

A helicopter is powered by horizontally rotating blades called rotors. The first working helicopter was built in 1939.

Da Vinci's drawing of his "aerial screw" flying machine. Experts think it would have taken more energy to fly than an operator could have produced.

As early as 400 BCE, people understood the principles of **vertical flight**. They made bamboo flying toys from a stick with a rotor attached, and they rolled the stick between their hands to launch it. About one thousand years later, Leonardo da Vinci drew plans for a flying machine with a turning spiral blade.

In the late nineteenth century, engineers invented devices to achieve vertical flight. However, it was only near the start of World War II that the first helicopters were built. In 1939 the Sikorsky Company in the United States built the first helicopter. More than 400 helicopters were used in World War II, mainly for search and rescue in the jungles of Southeast Asia.

VERSATILE MACHINES

Military helicopters have become more common since World War II. Larger helicopters have two rotors instead of one.

Igor Sikorsky (1889–1972) was a Russian-American aeronautics engineer. In 1939 he developed the first helicopter after he was inspired by the drawings of Leonardo da Vinci. Sikorsky's VS-300 was the model for all modern helicopters. In 1941 Sikorsky was asked to build the first military helicopters for the US Army Air Corps.

Igor Sikorsky flies a VS-300 helicopter. A small vertical rotor on the helicopter's tail prevents the aircraft from spinning around from the force of the main rotors.

VTOL Technology

A vertical takeoff and landing (VTOL) aircraft rises straight into the air and can also hover, like a helicopter. The most famous VTOL aircraft is the British Harrier Jump Jet. The Harrier has a single jet engine with four nozzles. The nozzles direct the thrust force downward for takeoff. When the jet is in the air, the nozzles turn to provide forward thrust for flight.

Helicopters transport people and supplies in areas with poor roads, and they evacuate wounded soldiers from the battlefield. Soldiers in helicopters fly above enemy locations to gather information. Helicopter **gunships** are also used in combat. The US Army used attack helicopters during the Vietnam War (1955–1975). They included the fast and heavily armed Bell AH-1 Cobra.

A helicopter hovers above rough ground. US soldiers jump out to begin a patrol in enemy territory during the Vietnam War.

This helicopter saw heavy action in 1968 during the Tet Offensive, a serious attack by the enemy on US targets throughout Vietnam.

An AH-64 Apache fires its missiles during a training exercise. The missiles can be guided to targets on the ground by following laser beams.

LATER CONFLICTS

US military helicopters were used again during later conflicts. In the first Gulf War (1990–1991), US forces and their allies drove Iraqi troops from Kuwait in the Persian Gulf in the Middle East. US Boeing AH-64 Apache helicopters led the invasion of Kuwait in Operation Desert Storm. Apaches fired the first shots of the war, destroying enemy radar and missile sites.

MILITARY TRANSPORTATION

Battlefield technology is not only about weapons. Technology also provides methods of efficient transportation for troops, supplies, and equipment.

In the middle of the nineteenth century, armies began to use railroads to move men and supplies. During the Siege of Sevastopol in the Crimean War (1853–1856), the British built a railroad just for their troops. Railroads were also important during the US Civil War. The Union had more railroads than the Confederacy, so Union commanders could move their troops quickly to more destinations.

SCIENCE FILE

Jeeps

The Willys MB was built in 1941 as a battlefield utility vehicle for the US Army. It was commonly known as a jeep. It was officially called a GP, or government purpose vehicle. US factories produced nearly 600,000 jeeps between 1941 and 1968. They were used in wars in Korea and Vietnam.

US Marines ride a train toward the front lines in France during World War I.

TWENTIETH CENTURY

In World War I, armies used railroads to move troops. And motor vehicles transported soldiers and supplies for the first time. But trucks often got stuck on muddy roads. World War II saw more use of tracked vehicles and small jeeps

On the modern battlefield, supply vehicles include transporters that carry tanks. In Afghanistan since 2001, US forces use all-terrain vehicles (ATVs) to get around. The ATVs pull trailers of supplies in areas with no roads.

The Humvee has a maximum speed of 70 mph (113 km/h). It has four-wheel drive, so it can operate in rough terrain.

Humvees

Humvee is the nickname of the High Mobility Multipurpose Wheeled Vehicle (HMMWV). The Humvee was built for the US Army in 1984. It was used to transport people and cargo. It was first used in combat in the US invasion of Panama in 1989. The Humvee was also used during the Gulf War.

HOVERCRAFTS

A hovercraft uses air pressure to float. That means it can travel over land, sea, ice, or mud.

The idea of the hovercraft first appeared in the early eighteenth century. British mechanical engineer Christopher Cockerell built the first working model in 1956.

A hovercraft uses blowers to pump air into a skirt below the body of the vehicle to create high pressure. The difference between the higher pressure underneath the vehicle and the lower

The Zubr-class LCAC is the largest hovercraft in the world. It has a maximum speed of 63 knots (72.5 mph, or 116.6 km/h).

The Polaris MRZR 4 Off-Road Vehicle is an American ATV. It can carry four soldiers plus supplies or six soldiers. It can also pull a cargo trailer.

pressure above lifts the craft off the ground. Propellers in the back of the craft provide forward motion.

The hovercraft was first widely used in combat by the US Navy during the Vietnam War. It was useful for traveling over the rivers and flooded rice fields in Vietnam's Mekong Delta.

WORLD'S LARGEST

The world's largest hovercraft is the Ukrainian-built Zubr-class LCAC (Landing Craft, Air Cushioned). The navies of Russia, Greece, and China use the LCAC. These craft are immense and powerful. It will be amazing to see how engineers continue to develop battle machines for the future.

All Terrain Transportation

Military ATVs have been widely used in recent conflicts in the Middle East. They can travel over rocky hills and sandy deserts. Small two- and four-seater ATVs can be transported by helicopter and dropped from the air. They are often used by members of the special forces.

TIMELINE

c. 500 BCE   Chinese engineers develop the trebuchet. This large catapult can throw balls of rock up to 410 feet (125 m).

c. 340 BCE   The Macedonians of ancient Greece develop the first siege catapult.

c. 800 BCE   Gunpowder is invented in China.

1415   At the Battle of Agincourt, English archers use powerful longbows to defeat a French army between five and ten times larger.

1780   The Sultan of Mysore in India successfully uses rocket artillery against the British East India Company.

1775   US inventor David Bushnell designs a submarine named the *Turtle* to destroy British ships during the Revolutionary War.

1851   The first machine guns appear. Both the Belgian mitrailleuse and the US Gatling Gun have mutiple barrels.

1862   Union engineers launch the USS *Monitor*, the first ironclad warship, in New York City.

1906   Britain launches HMS *Dreadnought*, the first battleship.

1909   Hiram Percy Maxim develops the gun silencer.

1915	The Dutch aircraft engineer Anthony Fokker introduces interrupter gear. It fires bullets through the propeller of a fighter plane.
1916	The British army introduces the first tanks in World War I.
1942	British engineer Barnes Wallace develops the "bouncing bomb," used by the Allied Forces to attack the Ruhr Valley in Germany's industrial heartland.
1942	The Germans fire V-2 rockets in long-distance attacks on London.
1945	On August 6 a US bomber drops an atomic bomb on the Japanese city of Hiroshima, starting a new age of nuclear weaponry.
1960	US engineer Theodore H. Maiman builds the first laser. Engineers use the laser to target missiles and as an alternative to radar.
1967	British engineers launch the Harrier Jump Jet, the only successful VTOL aircraft.
2013	British engineers design the Long Endurance Multi-Intelligence Vehicle (LEMV), a remotely piloted airship used to gather information about enemy positions.

GLOSSARY

airships: long, thin balloons powered by engines

Allied: describes the United States, Britain, and the Soviet Union in World War II

artillery: large guns such as cannons

barracks: buildings where soldiers live

communist: describes a political system in which everything is owned by the state

dogfight: a midair fight between fighter planes

forges: places where blacksmiths heat and shape metal into objects

fortifications: walls and barriers built to defend a place from attack

gunships: heavily armed helicopters

maneuver: to steer carefully

missiles: weapons that are propelled toward a target

multi-decked: having a number of stacked decks

obsolete: out of date

pressurized: having artificially high pressure

propellers: devices with turning blades that propel ships or aircraft

reinforcements: extra personnel to increase the strength of an army

steam engines: engines driven by the power of steam from heated water

surveyor: a person who carefully examines the land or buildings

vertical flight: flight in which an aircraft takes off and lands by moving straight up or down

FURTHER RESOURCES

Books

Burgan, Michael. *Weapons Technology: Science, Technology, and Engineering.* New York: Children's Press, 2017.

Oxlade, Chris. *Inside Fighter Planes.* Minneapolis: Hungry Tomato, 2018.

Perritano, John and James Spears. *National Geographic Kids: Everything Battles*. Washington, DC: National Geographic Kids, 2013.

Samuels, Charlie. *Machines and Weaponry of World War I.* New York: Gareth Stevens Publishing, 2013.

Websites

Ancient Greeks: Sea and Ships
http://www.bbc.co.uk/schools /primaryhistory/ancient_greeks /sea_and_ships/

A History of the Tank: From Leonardo da Vinci to the Second World War
http://www.telegraph.co.uk /sponsored/culture/film-fury /11146708/tank-history.html

Leonardo da Vinci Inventions
http://www.da-vinci-inventions .com/

Medieval Siege Tactics
http://www.timeref.com/castles /castsiege.htm

World War I: Aviation and Aircraft of WWI
http://www.ducksters.com /history/world_war_i/aviation _and_aircraft_of_ww1.php

INDEX